LOST IN MINECRAFT: A TALE OF ADVENTURE

A MINECRAFT NOVEL

Table of Contents

The Will

The world is a sandbox, and I, a lonesome shovel. In this expanse, I am both alpha and omega. Vulnerable against the elements conspiring against me, and at the same time, I conjure them. In the most painfully ironic fashion, time had lost its value to me a very long time ago. The seconds, days, months and eons have all smeared upon one another like a child's finger painting on the ether of the universe. I do not operate in a manner of seconds. I operate by the light of day and dark of night. "Day" and "night" may only be remnants of a period from when I could actually rise and sleep of my own will, when the calendar marked days that were special and days that were not. I can't recall the last time that I was able to freely perceive and adhere to my idea of time, though I suppose it changed when I became one with The Will. The Will compels me. I cannot recall when I first became an envoy of The Will, though that may be due to the fact that It does not wish for me to know so. The Will gives me a burning purpose that is anything but my own. You could say that It robbed me of what the people I once knew called "life." On the other hand, when light slowly recedes over the polygonal horizon and darkness reigns, The Will keeps me alive.

Or at least, it has so far.

The Will protects me from Them. They're unlike any other fashion of organism or entity I can imagine of my own accord. The Will does not enlighten me as to exactly what They are, but it urges me to avoid Them at all cost. They are a morbid fusion between alien and denizen of this world; in one instance seeming to be both an element of the surroundings and something entirely foreign to it. Their carapaces, perpetually alight with a sickly neon green that pierces the dark and shuns the light. Their movements, so devoid of reason and yet somehow filled with purpose; that purpose being to advance upon me. Their visages, contorted into a permanent Rorschach of blackened depressions that almost morbidly resemble what could be interpreted as a face.

In other words, they're pretty creepy. I've affectionately given them the title of "Creepers."

I do not know if The Will compels Them to pursue me at the same time that it compels me to flee Them, like some twisted pastime of an eternally bored deity. Whatever the case, It hasn't decided to make me a victim of Their advances yet. For the time being, It merely commands me, with a voice quieter than my own breath, to survive and build.

Like a moth that conjures the flame, my purpose is both my power and my constant undoing. I was put here to do but one thing—construct. Every angle of this never-ending expanse has known the life-giving strike of my hand. I am both the master of my domain and my own jailer.

And I'm pretty good with a pickaxe, too.

There's no telling just what The Will compels me to complete by the time my work here is done, provided that there is any sort of end in sight at all. Was I chosen for a reason, or am I only the latest or first of many? Am I part of a production line that discards obsolete products when they can no longer function? I'd like to know the answer to these, maybe even find out on my own accord. Unfortunately, the extent of my will seems to be rumination. My mind, ever curious, rotates on the swivel of an unfeeling axis that is my body; I think, it acts on a different agenda. This out-of-body experience has lasted for longer than I can remember when my thoughts and actions were one, before The Will brought me here to build Its blocky empire.

Blocks

Every single expanse of the world around me is littered with block in infinitum. Only six, simple sides compose each of them, and yet their potential to take on shape when put together is so hauntingly complex. I'd like to believe that within each of these little blocks, made of all colors not in the rainbow, there lies a wicked little bit of irony. For all of their maddening simplicity, they are now my all and everything. All the faculties of abstract thought and complex planning became obsolete when the blocks became my universe. Though some may seem to be stacked "high" or "low," it truly feels more like each of them orbits around me. I am the planetary impetus that compels these blocks to take their space in the world, and yet without them, I serve no purpose whatsoever.

Once upon a time, I attempted to keep count of all of the blocks that I'd erected in the name of The Will.

That didn't last long.

I've likely laid out enough of these cubes to fill out a space equal to the distance that I and every one of my ancestors, combined, has ever walked. And I have no way of telling if I'm even close to a quarter finished with the job yet.

In a comforting and yet painfully sobering kind of way, I've grown attached to them.

The Will gives me orders, yet the blocks give me purpose. Tending to the clockwork-like need to continue building, day-in and day-out, has become the pedestal that I stand upon to face my desire for answers. "Why?" Blocks. "What?" Blocks. "When?" Whenever there are blocks.

I am comforted in the feeling of having this great, overwhelming purpose. Just the feeling of having something, anything, to validate my stay on this unknown plane, is immensely cathartic.

And it forces me to face the reality that I've grown irreversibly mad. I should be desperate. I should be using every iota of strength in the recesses of my mind to fight off the compulsion of The Will. I shouldn't pick up one more block at all. I should use whatever resources I have to escape this predicament.

And yet, I do not.

I've stopped desiring it.

When the blocks became my purpose, they became my escape; that being the case, I escaped this place several lifetimes ago.

And I never looked back.

The Battle

The Will compels me to take a slightly different route this day. Instead of taking a stroll several-thousand feet below the ocean, I've been compelled to construct some peculiar companions.

The term "companion" is used sparingly, of course. I highly doubt that these companions that join me now, largely made out of the same material composing the surrounding landscape, are familiar with the higher echelons of sentience and critical thought.

Their forms are not as grotesque as my blotch-faced pursuers, but they are just as much alien from any comprehension I may have of what is natural. As far as naturalism is even concerned, I'm tempted to say that "natural" no longer has any meaning, so long as I am in this place.

The two of them together, a golem and a brute. The golem's skin takes a shade not unlike the deep grasp of midnight, every harsh angle of his profile like a slash of pure darkness scarred in the very air. Its profile is like a jagged boulder rolled from the very fabric of the spacial void. I made the behemoth with two mighty arms, segmented into hefty blocks with enough power to redecorate the landscape.

The brute was the golem's brother and antagonist. Rather than a nightshade-colored rock, this brute was with a body of pure ivory. He was not as stout as the golem, slightly taller and more trim. I made him in the form of a humanoid with primate-like features, though as for the exact reason why, I only wish I could say. The Will compels me, and I create; I created these two behemoths for only one reason: to do battle.

In the world that I used to inhabit, I have foggy memories of historical texts that detailed a particularly brutal ritual. My ancestors, however long they lived, created a grand spectacle out of organized combat. An entire era was defined by confrontation and physical subjugation; men and women from every walk of life would gather in a large structure called a Coliseum, and within it, they would validate their lives by fighting not to have it taken.

I built a similar vessel for my two, perpetually-at-war behemoth sons. In a twisted sort of way, my organization of their conflict was as methodical as a diligent father's care. Their mutual aggression and pain, if they could feel it, was like clockwork; and I, the craftsman that put the second and minute hands in place to begin with.

It was a gruesome display, but it alleviated the reality that threatened to surface every now and then; the reality of overwhelming, crushing boredom. For all the possibility that lie in the many blocks, there was an eerier aura of nothingness to this place. This infinity is an optimistic interpretation of the void.

In the heat of the golem and brute's conflict, though, there are real stakes. There is tension, uncertainty, a real sense of impending closure within the microcosmic timeline of their struggle. By arranging their battle, I arrange a single molecule of "purpose" in this infinite blocky miasma. For every blow that the golem lands on the brute, a resounding explosion of conviction and validations resonates through the air of this unending expanse. I have no way of knowing whether or not this is my own legitimate enjoyment or some form of corruption by The Will, but whatever the case may be, it is the way that things are for now.

The Explosion

Mistakes.

It just may be that for all of the real power possessed by the unknown impetus moving my body to act, it is not without some capacity for flaws.

Today, I was forced to come face-to-face with the consequences of a mistake.

Today, I became reacquainted with an old friend that hasn't so much as stopped in for tea in an untold amount of years.

The friend's name is mortality. Rather than calling, my good friend preferred to sidle up to my rear-left side and squeeze out a venomous hiss.

I had been surveying the shoreline for supplies, and in my search, I must have had taken longer than the timeframe I'd conditioned myself to adhere to. My internal body clock had slacked, and thanks to that, my external body would suffer.

The smell of stale butane and thick smoke briefly seized my nose like a thief in the dead of night, not even a single bit of warning or context included. The next moment can only be described in the way one would describe a blurry Polaroid picture.

As soon as the smoky stench had infiltrated my nostrils, I immediately felt my outer left side violently charge into my right insides. My heart at once felt as though it had a bass string run through it, and it felt as though that string had just been plucked by the heaviest fingers in the world. For a moment, my eyes gazed into the back of my own head.

So contorted was my sense of being that it almost felt like an extended out-of-body-experience. All of a sudden, as the Polaroid of vision came into focus and increased in resolution, I recognized the ground before it met my brow with savage impact. The out-of-body-experience became one that was agonizingly in-body, and within my body, there was a pain so great that it felt surreal.

It was the kind of pain that temporarily took all other senses hostage and assumed control over all forms of perception. Hearing hurt. Breathing hurt. My eyes were seeing things that my mind could not process and identify due to a preoccupation with the pain. I'm sure that if there were enough sensory flexibility left in my body, I would smell the pungent stench of heavy burning, too.

My most persistent and formidable adversaries on this plane, the Creepers, make self-preservation a trial; however, self-preservation is anything but on the top of their list of priorities. Aliens to even the other hostile organisms shambling about my territory, these monsters did not attack out of defense. Instead, they would stalk my footsteps like cats beneath the moon, before exploding with the vitality of three suns.

I had seen it before.

Not too long ago there was another here that shared my plight. He was… an impulsive sort of individual. He was not all that concerned with the most basic necessities for survival. Rather than harvest trees for wood and supplies, he could amuse himself for hours by building wooden crates and breaking them.

Every single crate broke apart as predictably as the last, and just as predictably, he would laugh and laugh, as if he'd chanced upon enlightenment.

To this day, I cannot decide whether or not he was driven completely mad or simply had this place figured out much better than I could have ever hoped to. Whatever the case may have been, he would follow this routine day-in and day-out until, one day, he no longer could.

He no longer could, due to the fact that he was incinerated without a trace.

I had seen it coming. A green tower of loathsome violence, sliding about the grassy knolls in the night as silently as an afterthought and as menacingly as a dreadnought. I must have yelled something to him, but he was too preoccupied with his precious crate.

It was almost darkly comedic. He brought his axe down to break the crate, and almost without a second's delay, he was blown to pieces. The night sky was illuminated in a brilliant flash of violent red and orange, and just like that, he and his attacker were no more.

Some days I wonder whether or not it was what he wished all along. In this place, all things are built and eventually destroyed. I build to create, I create to re-create. In his ritual of box-breaking and laughing like a madman, was he not simply doing exactly what I still do to this day, and enjoying himself? Had he become so a part of his surroundings that The Will compelled him to be destroyed just as another component of the environment?

If that is truly the case, then I thank my lucky stars that I've not become that strongly integrated into this place yet. Though my body works day-in and day-out to build these things, I've got no recollection of being attached to them. I am very much an alien under its atmosphere. The Creepers chase, I escape unscathed. The brute and golem do battle and I observe. The sun falls, I retreat underground. It rises and I with it. As time goes on, so will I. I don't know where or when, but whatever it is, I will.

The Gathering

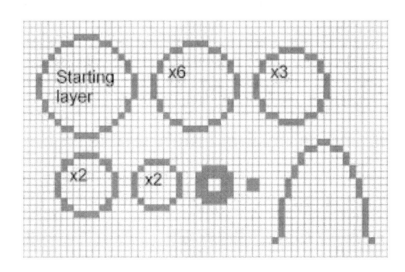

I have a plan.

In order to make this plan work in the slightest, I'm going to have to gather. Quickly, carefully and thoroughly. My time here has given me a powerful ability to make mental lists and execute in accordance to a schedule, and now, I will use those abilities to my greatest advantage.

The Will has compelled me to collect and build, and I have long since stopped resolving to resist Its command. However, in spite of this, I am not without conviction.

If I am ever to escape this polygonal domain and return to the place that I once called a homeland, then I'm going to have to play by the rules. I will not stop adhering to what The Will compels me to do, but at the same time, there will be a new end to these means. I will form a way to take the very fabric of this universe and use it as a tunnel of egress. This place has a sun and a moon, meaning it must operate based on some fundamental laws of physics. If that is the case, then it means that I was brought here by tangible means. I don't remember my name or upbringing, but my knowledge of the world makes it clear that I've not been completely severed from whence I've been taken.

Why would The Will abduct me and yet leave these faint memories of another place, another civilization, another form of existence completely apart from Its commands intact? Could it be that for all of Its power, It still has imperfections? Could this really be no more than a faint glitch in the system, a corrupted pixel in the programming that just may allow me to clip through?

Whatever it is, I will not protest the fact that it is here. I will continue to collect, gather, roam and survey the environment, but with new eyes.

These eyes will see through the dark nights and perilous landscape. They will see a future and a new beginning. In order to make this a reality, I'll need to utilize every skill that I've learned here to the fullest. I will need raw metal, I will need fuel, a source of energy, and above all else, time.

Time is the most important supply at my disposal. Time is also, thankfully, the asset that I have the fullest abundance of. I used to curse the abundance of time, but now I cherish it as much as the food that gives me strength to run from untimely death. I have time, I have a plan and I have infinite resources. If I cannot make my escape dream a reality with all of these tools at my disposal, then surely, it must have never been meant to be at all. If I cannot realize my plan without every step laid out before me, then how can I possibly call myself a captain?

...Captain.

That title rings a faint bell...and the tone is far more familiar than simply something I'd associate with any other word I know. It feels like...an identity. Captain.

That's right. I used to be a captain. And then...this.

The Eye of Iron

Not too far from where I've established my headquarters, there's a place that's ideal for collecting raw metal. It's an odd sort of land formation, a spiral-shaped abscess that spins downward into a pile of metallic scraps. From the right angle, the spiral and deposit of scraps resemble a massive, unblinking eye. The Eye of Iron.

Now that my eyes see the possibility of escape instead of an eternity trapped in subjugation, it is only appropriate that the Eye of Iron be my first place to begin the plan. I gingerly make my descent into the spiral, one tepid step at a time; being too reckless could easily bring everything to an end, but moving without enough urgency would force me to resurface from the Eye after sundown. With measured speed, I take the lengthy trek down into the iris of the eye as gingerly as I can.

After only a couple tense minutes of descent, I'm alarmed by a jagged, dragging sound. Just a couple of tiers beneath the ring of the eye I stand on, I have some unexpected company. Its face is white with the sort of paleness that far transcends human sickliness; it is an opaque face of ivory that can only be made out of pure bone. Where there would be eyes, there are but two pitch black recesses. If eyes are truly windows into the soul, then the Eye of Iron is a window into reclaiming my own soul, and this *thing's* eyes are windows into something that is far, far gone. Its body seems to function more like a vessel that's given impetus by something dearly wishing to escape it, the movements as unsynchronized and laborious as seizure spasms. Its epidermis seems more like a snow-speckled carapace, and closer inspection reveals that this, too, is made of bone. It's a corrupted portrait of something that may have once shared the same species as myself, but now, is cursed to roam until the end of time.

I did not expect to have to duel any skeletons on my descent, but I had much less expected to have an easy time of it. I raise my pickaxe with a tense and grim readiness, replacing my hopes for a tomorrow with gritty conviction. I edge closer down the spiral surface, dragging my foot just harshly enough to get the white ghoul's attention. The snap of its neck and head alerts me to the fact that I've gotten its recognition, and its entire demeanor instantly changes. Its movements become more purposeful, its limbs reach out to me with a yearning for contact, and if there were pupils in its dark recesses for eyes, I'd swear they would be as dilated as dinner plates.

I do not falter. It steps upward and I lurch downwards in anticipation. It raises a bony, clawed hand and I position my pickaxe for an upward slash. It brings its sharp digits down to land on my flesh, and the edge of my metal tool finds a home in its neck.

Recollections

Hauling the metal deposits up from the center of the Eye of Iron turned out to be even more perilous than the trip down. Not taking care to keep my cargo secure on the return trip would all but guarantee that the entire expedition would have been a waste. The skeleton that I'd put an end to on the way down had not been a lone ranger; as if on cue, after I had dispatched him, his cohorts seemed to crawl out of the woodwork.

My adrenaline felt like gasoline in the veins, and almost as if it were choreographed, I danced a ballad of un-death through droves of other skeletons that charged their way up to my descending position.

I'm unfamiliar with where my natural readiness with using the pickaxe as a combat tool came from; I've used it so much in this world that it does feel like an extension of my body, yet I cannot remember ever being an apprentice in any school for mining tool-based combat.

Now, combat in and of itself seems to hold some kind of strange fire for me. Though The Will dictates my thoughts, which command my body to build random things, my body has certain reactions to stimuli that seem all too familiar. The evasion of strikes with malicious intent, the counter stance, and the counter-strike, and the coup de grace. These feelings of the defiance of violence and resultant victory resonate throughout my mind like a vignette I've viewed millions of times before.

Almost as if they're formed from a memory.

The term "captain." Memories of combat. A dispute, a struggle, a kill, and suddenly, static.

These ruminations will have to be more closely examined at a later time. For now, I have all of the metal that I need and I can sense the emergence of Creepers from afar. I retreat to the hovel that I've dug for myself as a shelter, and sit down with an odd combination of tension and relief. I'm unsure of where my sense of extreme comfort and familiarity with combat have come from, but more importantly, I'm closer to a point at which I'll never have to concern myself with such things again.

I'll have my answers, my catharsis, my escape and my life back. The word "life" gives me a strange sensation as I realize it hasn't crossed my mind in ages. "Life's" definition took on a new meaning here, and it became more like the word "routine." Schedule, obligation, preparation and execution. When I use my gatherings to return to the world that I left, will the "life" that awaits me have the same rush of urgency?

The skeletons that attacked me were not alive, yet their movements spoke of conviction. Their purpose was to attack intruders, and they followed that through until I made them meet their ends. There's a macabre kind of admirableness in that.

The Hunter and the Hunted

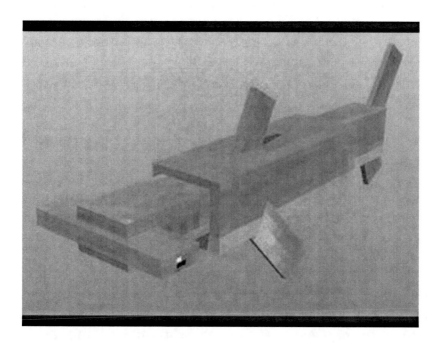

My work is tiresome, but my drive is tireless. Gone is the grip of The Will, and now there is only progress. My project has taken me from the Eye of Iron to the outskirts of the ocean. The voyage that I have in mind will require a significant amount of sustenance, and so I've made it a point to gather as many survival commodities as possible. With a hand-crafted spear, I jab at the mouth of the great blue and retract with it another scaly token of hope for survival. The jab of the spearhead ends each fish's struggle instantly and painlessly, and with their releases, I more anxiously await my own. Whereas before I was consumed with a sense of general aimlessness and obligation, now, there was purpose. A drive against inevitability, a push against impending failure, a reason to press onward; the vastness of the ocean makes me yearn to see the openness of what may wait beyond this place, and with it, perhaps a way to find answers.

My ruminations are brought to a screeching halt by a sudden electric jolt that makes my teeth chatter. For a brief point in time, the fishing boat I've constructed is completely divorced from the ocean's surface and crashes back down with a deafening roar of disturbed water. Salty tears of ocean drops pitter-patter down around in a wide radius, and I briefly lament the fact that the some of the fish I've collected have been thrown over my vessel's edge.

I've got little time to make sense of what's occurred before the impact rocks my boat again, this time with even more vigor than before. I'm able to use my spear and brace against the momentum of the crash to avoid being thrown completely overboard, though not before half of the boat is overrun with a surge of water. Even in the white obfuscation of crashing water, I catch a glimpse of my tormentor.

Like all things in this world, its profile is made up completely of cubic partitions and sharp angles. The body is thick, tapering off into a thinner end that is then split off into two axe-like protrusions. The opposite end of the beast vaguely resembles the edge of a fat bullet, and on its underside, a small opening that reveals multiple rows of sharp, whitened edges.

My aggressor is a massive hammerhead shark, and for whatever reason, it does not approve at all of my endeavors. With one final ram making the world spin, I'm soundly motivated to prevent any further interaction with the marine enforcer. I steady myself on the opposite edge of my vessel, taking note of the fish that still compose my collections for the day; my objective was to gather food, not to do battle with an oceanic bully, but the priorities have changed. He raises his head from the murk of the ocean bears a row of ivory spears in his mouth. I grit my teeth and steady my pole arm, aiming my single spearhead to face his several dozen. With no more time for deliberation, I feel the blocks in my arm twitch before they spring forth like water from a pressure cooker, sending the spear out to greet my aggressive guest.

It sounds like a stake being driven through a sheet of metal, which momentarily catches me off-guard. My assailant is made of something far harder than I anticipated, and before I can properly digest that fact, I'm face-to-dorsal fin with it. For the first time in a long time, I am forced to thank The Will for making me act. By only a hair's length, I'm able to dodge the razor sharp edge of the fin that rends my fishing boat in two. I'm caught in the shortest and yet longest feeling of weightlessness in my life before my back hits the salty brine of the ocean, and my vision becomes nothing more than a blue gradient. Resurfacing from the grip of the sea, eyes peppered with little liquid comets, I once again face my persistent assailant. As opposed to before, I'm overcome with a far deeper sense of dread. With my feet no longer on a solid surface, I must face the fact that I'm now in my opponent's element instead of my own. The ruler of the ocean refused to accept my declination of his invitation, and so now, I am forcibly welcomed to his domain.

The feeling of legs seems like little more than cruel joke to remind me that they're useless in avoiding attack; however, the grip on my spear has not loosened since I was thrown into the mouth of the ocean. Moving with the low speed of something painfully separated from its element, I ready my spear to face the advancing leviathan. With little to no ability to wield it as effectively underwater as I would in the open air, I instead resolve to move my own body as effectively as I can. When the beast lunges once more, I brace for impact and kick as strongly as possible to get out of the way.

I feel the spear's handle violently rattle in my hand as the impact is made. My hand is shocked into numbness by the smashing blow, and electricity resonates through my forearm and up into my shoulder blade. My body remains unbitten, though the blunt force is enough to make the world temporarily go white. The spearhead harshly grazed the shark's side and managed to liberate a generous amount of flesh. Blocks from the wounded area drift off into the distance of the ocean, as listlessly as snowfall, but my attacker is anything but placid. The pain fires off every nerve that commands the beast to do battle, and at this point, I know I'm in for nothing short of a genuine struggle. I only pray that by the struggle's conclusion, I'm able to escape with at least my more coordinated limbs.

The beast recoils for a minute, but doesn't drop a single percent of its unbridled rage. As soon as it has regained its composure, it races back at me like a savage torpedo. With nothing less than all of the nerves in my body that can be summoned, I ready the spear once more.

The beast comes at me with feverish intensity, and I solemnly bite back my lip in anticipation of the clash. In less time than I can bat an eyelash, the impact strikes again. I'm helpless against the push of an iron wall of gnashed spear teeth ramming into the edge of my weapon, and before I know it, my feet are being driven into the soggy marsh of the ocean floor. The blood pressure leaves my skull, and for a moment, I swear that the strength flees my arms entirely. All it takes is an electric jolt from the sudden shift in pressure on the spear to bring back every ounce of pressure and pain. The shark's mouth is pried open by only my spear's sharp edge, and just the slightest bit of leeway that I permit could result in immediate consequences.

I'm forced to make a critical decision. I can't continue to stronghold the multi-ton death fish for much longer, and even if I could, the Creepers would surely await me on the shore by nightfall.

I resolve to make what may be the most decisive and horribly uncalculated choice of my entire existence. Instead of pressing the spear harder into the shark's impregnable wall of sabre teeth, I pull it back and allow darkness to overcome me.

The shark's mouth is massive enough to almost completely engulf my upper body, and I can feel the stinging graze of serrated teeth raking across my shoulder blades. With my head and shoulders enveloped by the shark's maw and my feet still depressed into the ocean floor, it really does feel like the most literal interpretation of being caught between one world and the next.

I don't savor the feeling of limbo for long. With some vigorous tugging, I'm able to dislodge the spear's edge from the section of vital innards that it's pierced within my felled adversary. My gambit could have gone more than one way, and in this present moment, I'm only happy to still have a functioning body and mind. There was no guarantee that the jab was going to actually stop the shark, and it barely did, but The Will serves me well on this day.

With the underwater skirmish finally over, I can finally begin to make a slow ascension to the water's surface. I naturally expected to be relieved at no longer having to fight for my life beneath the waves, but it's a short-lived feeling. Surveying the damage to my boat is briefly an even worse feeling than the dread of imminent demise by shark. Almost every fish that I collected has been thrown from the hull, with only a few scaly cadavers littering the bottom as pitiful tokens of condolence. I escaped the jaws of death, but my jaws of life have temporarily been disabled. With all the enthusiasm of a wet cat, I stroke over to the battered boat and clamber back into the bow. It will be another day that I have to collect food from the ocean, but no matter what, that day must come.

I could have wound up not returning from the ocean at all, but the fact that I have is a blessing that can't be taken lightly. I'm able to see that the sun is just about over the horizon, and because of this, chances are that I'm not going to make it back to my headquarters without some violent Creeper encounters. Whatever the case, this isn't a time to lament and lick my wounds. I've got enough fish collected in the boat to make it through the night and keep me running tomorrow, and so I'll just have to use the extra energy for a more successful quest.

The Thunderclap

As expected, tugging the small load of fish back from the shore to home base was not an easy endeavor. On the one hand, I was forced to acknowledge that the load was pitifully diminished from its former glory prior to the shark encounter. On the other hand, it may have been a blessing in the most unpleasant of disguises.

Creepers littered the landscape like ants on a sugar spill, and if I had been carrying a load any more impressive than the one I'd been forced to settle on, there would be no guarantee that I'd have had the speed to survive. In a way, the horde of Creepers was even more dangerous than the encounter with the shark had been. Their constant advances were easier to evade, and yet the aftermath was far more severe. Every step of my manic sprint kept me just a hair's length out of range of another explosion. Some of them got just close enough so that the blast wave from their kamikaze rush would completely take me off my toes before pile-driving me into another wet bed of soil.

Then the black cloud arrived.

When I had been out on the water, I had noticed a cumulonimbus forming a slight distance past the shoreline. I had disregarded it as something that would pass, but in the current context, it was far direr than I had ever imagined. The wind stung my face with the ferocity of intangible whips, and every cry of thunder resonated like the roar of a brutal slave driver. The lightning flashes would temporarily make the entire landscape become a shade of azure-tinted ivory, and in the distance, I could see the treetops temporarily catch light from a newborn blaze. The lightning itself wasn't of any real concern, but its effect was what truly demanded the most caution.

There's an extreme peculiarity to the Creeper physiology that's both amazing and horrifying. Occasionally, a strike of lighting would come perilously close to actually making contact with the Creepers themselves; almost as if the lightning was somehow drawn to their bodies by some form of alien electromagnetism. When this would happen, for some inconceivable reason, they would not be destroyed on the spot. By some bizarre chance, the lightning would not char their skin or damage their bodies in any way. Instead, their normally vibrant green skin would become radiant with a luminous, electric-blue hue. While the visual was admittedly beautiful, the reality was nothing short of absolutely terrifying. The Creeper, when charged with the essence of lightning, becomes a sort of sentient natural disaster. The waves of light emanating from a Creeper affected by lightning were a sign of unbridled, overwhelming and destructive energy. Normal Creepers would simply explode and cause significant discomfort from the burn, but a Charged Creeper was in a class all of its own.

I had spotted one near the back of a horde that charged me on my sprint from the shoreline, a pale slash of blue in a rolling sea of hostile green enemies. They were relentless, each of them, but the one consumed by flowing blue energy was decidedly more menacing. It was unclear just how he had been the only one unfortunate enough to get lightning-struck amongst all of his kin, but in the Creeper hive mind, individuality and cognition are not even sub-factors. Each of them had nothing less than the mission to end my life by explosively ending theirs; one of them just so happened to be much more fatal and proficient at their job than the rest.

With the small satchel of fish in hand, I made my bout for the hills more quickly than my mind even had time to assess the danger. Though they made no snarling, predatory sounds in their pursuit, the very premonition of what may happen if I wasn't fast enough was absolutely deafening. I could feel the familiar stomach-dropping pressure of a close-range explosion on my skin, I could see their sickly green shells even without directly looking at them, and I could even smell the faint burning aroma of kerosene that signaled their imminent arrival.

All of the senses activating at once led to a surreal feeling of both overstimulation and numbness; an out-of-body experience brought on from being completely trapped within every facet of the moment. I was so consumed by my fear that I no longer noticed it, like being trapped in the belly of a whale that you can't possibly see in its entirety. I was a machine in action, a messy line of poetry in frantic motion; The Will compelled me to run for dear life, and I did no less than that.

And then I tripped.

In my time spent in this bizarre plane of blocks and hostile demons, I can recount more than a couple times when I felt close to knocking on the door of eternity. However, as opposed to those times, this time I truly had no plan of action. My shovel made me adept at digging into the ground for a hasty retreat, but I was unprepared for the circumstance of going face-first into the ground instead of down into it. The creepers advanced without even a stutter step in surprise, completely and utterly unaffected by my mistake. They pressed on like machines, their momentum immutable, automatic and cold.

It became apparent that one of the machines operated with a much higher caliber engine than the rest. The lightning-charged Creeper, it's body irradiated with a wild blue wavelength of power, seemed to be overrun with a new degree of vitality. It was beginning to pull ahead of the pack, and in that instance, I became conscious of the fact that I was not moving at all. I was unable to summon the will to do anything but stare at the sheer, flooring imminence of it all, the pulse of an anxious heartbeat, the drumming pounding of fear coming into actualization, the hiss of the irradiated Creeper inching closer before it shone with blinding brilliance and all became nothing more than hard and burning light.

I don't know how much time had passed when I finally regained consciousness.

Aftershocks

There was a pounding in my skull that seemed like a giant's fist being rammed in the space behind my eyelids. A harsh jackhammer of electricity revved up and sparked down my spine with even the slightest movement. It seemed as though my body was no longer an entire piece; like it was actually a marionette, each component built separately, pulled together in the same general space with only the faintest bits of string.

Any attempt to rise from the ground would only create another silent tidal wave of flame in my core, and I was pulled down on my back in the soil by the gods of pain.

I was going nowhere fast, but I prayed that the feeling would subside more quickly than my inability to move.

All of the cardinal directions have virtually disappeared from my ability to perceive. The world was an amorphous, rotating swirl of push and pull that took several seconds to assume a full form, but when it did, it became apparent that the world had indeed changed.

I had been on a grassy knoll before the charged Creeper had exploded, but now, there was hardly a shred of green in sight. The area around had been reduced to a massive, bowl-like indention in the very face of the earth. What had been beneath my feet before was now over twenty feet above, and before me, pillars of crumbling sediment tumbled to the floor of the crevice like exhausted, ancient gods on their last failing legs.

I can feel my own heartbeat drumming slowly on the inside of my chest, like a weakened bird vying for escape from a rattle cage. As sensations begin to creep back into my veins, no longer numbed by the blast, the full realization of what's occurred becomes clear like a defogged window. The charged Creeper had exploded on a scale that made the others look like little more than firecrackers. In the past, explosions from the average Creeper would feel like a particularly hot and heavy tackle; this felt more like being hit by a flaming truck. I am far more than just lucky to be alive; it's downright inconceivable that I am. Perhaps due to either the unstable nature of the charged Creeper or plain dumb luck, the explosion had not gone off as close to my body as it could have. If the Creeper had been only a couple precious meters further, it's highly likely that I wouldn't even have a brain to conceive thoughts about the situation.

I had come back from the shore after narrowly escaping a skirmish with a shark. I had lost most of my bounty for the day, but I had managed to fend off the primal fish and take my much smaller fish ashore. I was swarmed by Creepers in the midst of a storm, and in the process of that chase, one of them that had been irradiated by lightning joined in on the pursuit. My guardian angels took their eyes off of me for a moment, and I tripped over my own feet. The charged Creeper had managed to break apart from the pack, pulsing with lightning, and exploded with the force of ten thunderclaps.

Now here I was, laid out at the bottom of what felt like a half-mile deep crater. My body felt as though it had been put through a titan-sized dish disposal and my food scraps may as well have been fossilized, but I had managed to twice defy death in less than one rise and fall of the sun; all things considered, being alive was a fine consolation.

For some odd reason, I couldn't shake the feeling of nostalgia, however. Never before had I ever had the feeling after a Creeper encounter, but in this instance, the feeling of being rocked to hell and back by a massive explosion made me feel as though I was living in a flashback. Being thrown off my feet and into the grip of nothing less than airborne chaos felt strangely familiar. I could almost sense the last time that it had happened, in a place so far away and yet close enough to feel emanations of heat. It's impossible to tell exactly when or where it occurred, but I could taste it on the tip of my tongue and feel it in my sore bone marrow.

Whether it was a matter of The Will or not, things were starting to seem strange. Considering the nature of the world I've called my dwelling for who knows how long, something peculiar had been awakened in the blast, like a piece of diamond shrapnel driven into my brain after the blast of a cosmic grenade.

The thrill of combat. The name, "Captain." A chain of command, those men at my command. A voyage, a storm, a setback and an explosion.

Tiny snippets of words that should hold meaning flitted through my brain like ephemeral dragonflies, each one disappearing just as swiftly as it appeared. I hadn't the faintest clue of how to connect them, but each of them seemed connected in the oddest way. A thread as vital as the Thread of Life spun by the fates of Greek mythology, so significant and yet completely ineffable. It was maddening, but my musings were immediately washed away by a tide of sobering realization; I still had a job to do.

My body felt as though it was being tugged by weak puppet strings as I rose from my prone position on the ground, the feeling of standing on two feet almost seeming like an entirely unfamiliar form of existence. My supplies were decimated, the sun was just barely peeking over the jagged mountain teeth on the horizon, and I was in poor shape.

The crater that I stood at the bottom of was immense, and there wasn't a single doubt in my mind that it would take more effort than I could muster at the present state to clamber out of. The walls of the massive indention in the earth were smothered in a thick coat of gray. Pools of soot and ash laid about the base of the earthen floor in impressive piles, each of them easily surpassing any average man in height. I walked by them with a mixture of admiration and despair; such destruction made possible only by the tantrum of one Creeper alone. How could a world with so much creation be marred by such unbridled and senseless destruction? Perhaps in this place, only complete and constant cataclysm can serve as a check for the infinite potential to build.

Build. I still had to construct my final project, and it required more than the steel I had already managed to pull together from the Eye of Iron. However, all of the land immediately before me was not exactly rich with materials I could use for an escape. The floor was ashen, the walls were ashen, and rays of light that pierced through the opening above and shone about parts of the crater only revealed even more depressed ash.

Some parts of the great, ashen bed let off faint glints that caught my eye. I kneeled down to more closely inspect one of these bright glints, and to my surprise, it turned out to be something of a small trinket. Circular in shape, with luminescent rays of color extending across its chrome surface along its circumference. I had to take a moment to appreciate the annoyingly perfect irony of it all. Even in the midst of total destruction, this world still manages to introduce something new and unfamiliar. I had no idea about the exact purpose of the disc, but it would not have been unearthed without my near-fatally explosive encounter.

The disc was, surprisingly, not charred in the slightest from the severity of the explosion that unearthed it. At the very worst, it was simply blemished by the same layers of soot and ash that filled the violently carved earth crater I stood in.

And then it hit me.

Something about the ash and soot was "off." It carried a distinct scent to it, like a waft of something pungent in a cloud of charcoal and dust. It was unidentifiable and unmistakable all at the same time; however, my nose wouldn't give me any more information that I pestered it for.

Perhaps The Will or something more deranged compelled me, but without a second thought, I scooped some of the newly-peculiar sediment from the disc and popped a lightly-coated finger between my lips.

Immediately, my mouth was overcome with the taste of metal. A distinct, metallic tang dance on my tongue that would have forced me to spit it out were it not for my immense surprise and relief.

Gunpowder. I had been in need of something more than only the raw materials and supplies that I'd gathered so far, and this was exactly the ticket. It took all of the self control I had not to take an entire handful of the explosive powder and scoop it into my mouth for a fuller taste. The thrill of having it in my hands was downright intoxicating, and now that it was here, it meant that the reality of success had become all the more within my grasp.

Completely gone was my regret about the decimated fish that I'd gathered earlier on. It felt as though an ocean of lead had been lifted off of my spine. The Eye of Iron had given me a near-infinite reservoir of metal to craft, and with this, I had a pool of virtually limitless combustible energy.

Not wasting a second more to reflect on this most undeserved of good fortune, I began to make a spirited climb out of the mouth of the crater. The loose soot on the walls slightly impeded my ascent, but with enough effort, I was able to overcome the uneven footing and reunite with sun-kissed ground.

The sky wore a different shade of blush than when I'd last seen her out on the water. Whereas before she had been a murky navy, she was now almost completely overcast. It may have been a combination of the storm's residual influence and the tower of debris that must have been upchucked from the blast. However, even in the thickness of the sky's occlusion, there were several golden needles that stuck through the underbelly of the clouds like a grand aerial pincushion.

The sun's skeletal fingers pierced through the thickness of ash, debris and black cloud with a combination of power and indifference; just looking at it gave me all of the resolve I needed to turn back in the direction of my shelter.

Once at the shelter, I waste no time in collecting my strongest shovel and wheelbarrow. Transporting all of the gunpowder that I need from the depths of the crater to my supply collection proves to be nothing short of a momentous task, but with the high of renewed volition coursing through my veins, each load feels positively lighter than air. I'm able to get about four loads of the ashen powder transported to my shelter before nightfall began to overtake the land once again, and I don't intend on chancing yet another jab at good fortune by being hit with another Creeper explosion. I retire into my subterranean hovel, surrounded by the inanimate fruits of my labor, and close my eyes to the kind of rest that can only be experienced after an immense struggle's closure.

The charged Creeper's blast had managed to bring more than just complete desolation. In fact, there seemed to be a slightly disturbing trend in the events that had transpired. The skirmishes in the Eye of Iron, the bloody bout with the belligerent shark, and the chase through the storm that had nearly finished me off for good, but only led to brand new beginnings.

It all seemed far too surreal. The fact that surrealism still had weight in this place that defied all laws of common sense and conservation gave me the oddest hope. Even with the infinite variables working against me, and several lifetimes spent basking in the madness of a block-built prison, there was still an inkling of something apart from it all that persevered. I was able to hold onto a shred of the part of me that just may have existed before I had ever come here, and the knowledge of that washed over me like a tide of holy water. The very world "holy" sparked a certain reaction in my mind that blossomed like an explosion in slow motion.

Holiness. Order. Law. Order. Command. Captain. Voyage. Skirmish. Betrayal. Explosion. Rebirth. Survival. Static.

Human.

The concepts of things so far from me, and yet at a place too close to measure, became overwhelming. Like dusting off books that had been fossilized at a time before time was measured. Yet, somehow, I had read them all before.

At that very moment, space itself took on a different meaning. I became conscious of something particularly unsettling.

This world itself, its very composition, was skewed. The shape of all things composing it, I realized, was horrifically limited. All things created with six sides and eight angles; they were perfect cubes. These cubes were the building blocks of my surroundings, but I knew there had to be more beyond only building blocks; more-so, I knew there had always been more than only building blocks constructing the fabric of the universe.

In this place I had been conditioned to believe that building blocks are all there is to any kind of matter at all, and in the process, I had forgotten the existence of others. To be reunited with the otherness of the world above, to finally regain a sense of what shapes exist beyond only blocks, my mission had to be successful. There was no other option.

And at that moment, The Will compelled me to move. Back to the shore, with tools in hand, building a small boat for the ocean as if nothing at all had happened. It compelled me to stoically row it out into the same square of seawater where I'd been attacked by the ferociously territorial sea beast, and there, I simply restarted my long-delayed fishing trip. Stinging, thirsty, beaten and yet completely undeterred, I dipped my line into the mouth of the vast ocean and counted to ten.

Acension

The supplies had finally been completely gathered. I had all of the metal I needed, all of the freeze-dried supplies I needed to last me indefinitely, and most importantly, enough gunpowder for lift-off.

The vessel I'd created was never plotted out on any kind of blueprint. In an odd kind of way, it seemed as though I'd always instinctually known the instructions.

Perhaps it was incorrect to say that I'd never had a blueprint to construct the vessel. Somewhere, I'm sure, in part of my past that was lost in translation, there must have been some extreme form of practiced efficiency. My muscles and digits moved with the kind of readiness that can't be learned, only tempered and sharpened from repeated practice over time.

As I gazed up at the final result of all of my work, I felt as though I was looking at a monument. Something that, moments before, had little to no representation in my mind or memories. Now, gazing upon it, the weight of its significance was like a pile of heavy and hot coals on the brain.

I'd outfitted it to be capable of transporting myself and all of my supplies. Its hull was unpainted, but it caught the reflections of the sunset on its chrome finish. The vessel was almost larger than the dwelling I'd been living in during the time I'd merely been a servant to The Will, but from now on, there was no telling how long it would be my new dwelling on the upcoming voyage.

I step up the stairs and into the ribs of the metal beast I've constructed; each click of my foot on the steps I'd built into the cockpit sounding like the tick of a clock counting down to revolution.

I'd kept the construction of the inside of the hull relatively Spartan, maximizing all utilities and lowering weight for maximum power during liftoff. My position at the helm of the vessel, before a wide pane of transparent glass to serve as my vision, gave a new spin on the world before me. Out there, at the mercy of the environment, this place was both my home and my prison. Now, in this vessel, it seems so bizarrely far apart that it's unsettling.

I saw the jagged teeth of mountain tops on the horizon. It had been on those very mountain tops that I'd first gained consciousness on this plain, and after an arduous descent, my first encounter with predatory Creepers. I had been forced to stop advancing after encountering the massive body of water at the mountain's base, and it had been there that The Will first compelled me to construct. I had built a small boat to cross over to the grassy hills where my shelter lie, and from that point on, I would continue to build and build without end. I had built more things than even a lifetime of ceaseless work could manage to memorize, but it both began and ended with the construction of a vessel. The first one was merely built to cross over the water, and this one, to traverse the starts.

The control panel should have been alien to me, but I was operating on the kind of autopilot that I'd grown accustomed to obeying without question. After strapping in and initiating some startup processes, I felt the hum of the vessel I built grow steadily louder. Though it was stored deep within the innermost faculties of the machine, I could almost hear the whirring of super-heated oxygen and fuel mixing together at high speed. The roar of the engine continued to escalate in attitude and pressure, and then, ignition.

It was a blast more titanic and severe than the charged Creeper's kamikaze assault. A dramatic and overwhelming pressure in my gut that sent my soul into the back of my seat, and the landscape before the pane of glass turning into a blurred watercolor painting before my very eyes.

For the longest time, I awaited oblivion. I expected something inside of The Will to conspire against my heresy, my insubordination, my blatant infidelity and unannounced divorce from Its grip. I could see the Coliseum I built below, becoming like an electron in the miasma of a large and square cell; I was only just beginning to move to another part of the body.

Before long, the pressure was gone, and there was a stillness. A feeling of levity that was more than only freedom, but also strongly physical; having broken out of orbit, beyond the pull of gravity, there was nothing to savor but the feeling of absolute victory.

Which was quickly replaced by a sudden premonition of panic. I had escaped the world of blocks, my vessel had reached orbit, and yet still, there were no answers. I would have no choice but to press all thrusters into the heart of the abyss, hoping that, eventually, I would reach somewhere that would give me a sign to the place I had once called home. The source of the firecracker flashes in my mind at the words "Captain," "crash," "combat" and "discovery." I glanced to the rear of the cockpit, eyeing a satchel I'd brought aboard to hold some tools that just may have been useful in a pinch; some functional, some fundamental.

I would have no need for a shovel in the grip of space, but somehow I'd felt compelled to bring it along. In addition to that shovel, I kept the disc-shaped totem I'd come across at the bottom of the crater.

I couldn't put my finger on it, but something was urging me. It urged me to retrieve the disc from the satchel. There was something, but I didn't know what. Something out in the vastness of the ether that would give me answers, linked to this disc.

And I would have to build it. I had the will to build it.

My vessel made an aimless course through the void, betwixt titanic rock formations in the cosmos. Each of the rocks shared a peculiar, square shape.

Bonus Section

Thank you for reading this book. I hope you enjoyed it. Gaming is very near and dear to my heart and I enjoy every moment I spend playing my favourite games.

If you liked this book, and are interested in more, I invite you to join my "Customer Only" newsletter at http://awesomeguides.net/. I publish all my best stuff there for free, only for my customers.

If you're a Minecraft fan like I am, I'm sure you'll like my other best-selling releases:

1. Minecraft: Awesome Building Ideas for You
2. Amazing Minecraft Secrets You Never Knew About
3. Minecraft All-In-One Quick Guide! Master your Minecraft skills in Everything!
4. The Amazing Tale of Steve: A Minecraft Novel
5. Minecraft: Amazing House Designs with step-by-step instruction
6. Awesome Minecraft Traps To Defend Your Home
7. 50 Awesome Minecraft Seeds That You NEED to Know
8. Amazing Minecraft Maps You Will Definitely Enjoy!
9. Minecraft Amazing Redstone Contraptions
10. The Ultimate Minecraft Guide to Tekkit: Discover the Advanced Mods for Minecraft!

In my strategy guides, I share neat tips and tricks to help you get better at gaming. From Candy Crush to Dragonvale, you'll find strategy guides for a wide variety of addictive games.

1. The Last of Us: Amazing Strategies and Secrets

2. <u>Dragonvale: The Complete Guide: Amazing Cheats, Gems, Breeding and MORE!</u>
3. <u>Candy Crush Saga Best Tips, Tricks and Cheats!</u>

We also have an awesome Minecraft course on Udemy – an instructor led online learning platform.

1. <u>All about Minecraft: A complete educational course</u>

Have fun gaming!
Egor

CPSIA information can be obtained at www.ICGtesting.com
Printed in the USA
LVOW13s1756170714

394812LV00021B/1178/P